Eating Feet

by Susan Manlin Katzman

❖

illustrated by Susan Stillman

Scott Foresman

Editorial Offices: Glenview, Illinois • New York, New York
Sales Offices: Reading, Massachusetts • Duluth, Georgia
Glenview, Illinois • Carrollton, Texas • Menlo Park, California

"Tony, what do you want to eat?"

Tony has three favorite foods. When his mom asks, he always says the same thing.

He says, "Elephant teeth, little worms, or wolf eyes, please."

He likes these dishes with tomato sauce.

Tony lives in Italy.

The teeth, worms, and eyes he likes so much are pastas. Pasta is a dough made of flour and water. The dough is made into different shapes.

Pasta is often named for its shape. *Spaghetti* means "long string." It looks like string too. Elephant teeth are tube-shaped. Little worms are long pieces of pasta. As you may have suspected, the pieces look like worms. Wolf eye pasta is small and round.

Teeth and worms and little eyes?
Surprise, surprise!
These foods are pastas in disguise!

5

6

Gwen lives in England. She always gets to eat what she wants on her birthday. Her dad cooks the meals.

Gwen always picks toad-in-the-hole for breakfast. She has bangers and mash for lunch.

Then it's bubble and squeak for dinner! Gwen thinks these foods are great.

Toad-in-the-hole is an old English dish. It is NOT made with real toads! It's pork sausages that look like toads. The sausages hide under a crust.

Bangers is a British word for "sausage." *Mash* is another British word. Can you guess what it means?

Right. It is just as you suspected. Gwen has mashed potatoes for lunch.

And what about bubble and squeak? Cooks in England fry potato and cabbage in a pan. The food bubbles when it cooks and makes a squeaky sound. So the dish is called bubble and squeak.

If your dinner squeaks and bubbles,
don't think that you have troubles.
Bubble and squeak is really good.
Try it once. You know you should!

Sasha is a Russian boy. His mom serves fish eggs at parties.

Kai lives in Japan, where raw fish is party food. Kai enjoys all kinds of raw seafood. She likes octopus the best.

Marc is from France. On special days, Marc gets to eat cheese with blue, moldy streaks through it.

Many Chinese boys and girls want to eat chicken feet for their special meals.

Some party food is so good, it has traveled from one country to others. Russian fish eggs are called *caviar*. (The word rhymes with "handlebar.") It is a food people around the world like to eat.

So is the Japanese raw fish called *sashimi*. (This one rhymes with "come see me.")

The first blue-mold cheese came from France. French immigrants brought it with them to America. Now blue cheese is made in many countries.

While chicken feet may not have found their way to your table yet, that doesn't mean they're not delicious! Many people in China and other countries eat this food.

Don't say no to something new.
You'll miss good food if you do.
You may find that fresh, raw fish
can become your favorite dish!

Pretend that you don't know anything about American food. What would you think if you heard that Americans eat hot dogs?

Dogs? Served hot?

What if you learned that kids like to chew on submarines and torpedoes? Weird!

What if someone offered you string beans? You might think they were made out of string! And what about sponge cake? You might not have suspected that it is a treat!

Each country has its own special food traditions. Food from one place may seem odd somewhere else.

Maybe the food is not well known. Maybe it just has a strange name.

Always keep an open mind. Foods are a lot like people. Most of them are just great when you get to know them.